Preschool Scissor Skills

Workbook

(Ages 3 to 5)

Featuring a variety of fine-motor skill activities for preschool children.

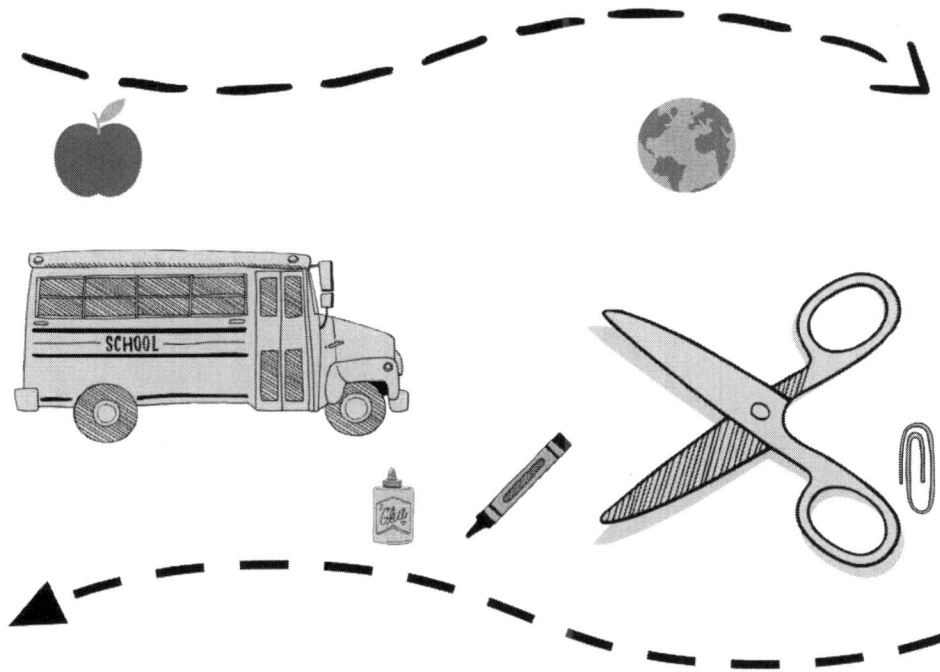

Kids World Journals and Books

How to Use this Book

Recommend Materials: Child-safe scissors, crayons, colored pencils, glue sticks or non-toxic glue, pencils and light water-based markers.

1). Encourage your child to use a pencil or crayon to trace around the dotted lines of a shape or an image inside the book.

2). Help your kids color the picture with their favorite crayons or colored pencils. Encourage them to color within the lines and take their time, but don't fuss if they scribble all over the page. It takes time to enhance fine-motor skills.

3). Tear out the page and help them create doodles of their own on the back of the page. Practice makes perfect! ☺

Drawing every day will help your child develop fine-motor skills and in time they will develop their own artistic style.

4). Help your child use scissors to carefully cut around the image.

5). Save your child's creations in an envelope for later use or help them glue their colored images on the blank pages in the back of the book. Kids can also use the pages at the back to draw anything they like or decorate this area with stickers.

Tips for Success

* Your child will be more likely to complete these projects, if you color with them and get excited about the process.

* Encourage your child to customize the book based on their own interests. For instance, you can decorate the back portion of the book with glitter heart stickers or colorful dinosaur stickers.

* Your child will most likely need extra help using scissors. Be sure to purchase scissors that are age appropriate for your child.

* Have FUN!! ☺

Create your own memory game

Color, cut and enjoy an animal ABC memory game

Antelope

Antelope

Bear

Bear

Camel

Camel

Deer

Deer

Elephant

Elephant

Fox

Fox

Giraffe

Giraffe

Horse

Horse

Iguana

Iguana

Jaguar

Jaguar

Kangaroo

Kangaroo

Lion

Lion

Mouse

Mouse

Nightingale

Nightingale

Orangutan

Orangutan

Pig

Pig

Quail

Quail

Rabbit

Rabbit

Sheep

Sheep

Tiger

Tiger

Unicorn

Unicorn

Vulture

Vulture

Whale

Whale

Xrayfish

Xrayfish

Yak

Yak

Zebra

Zebra

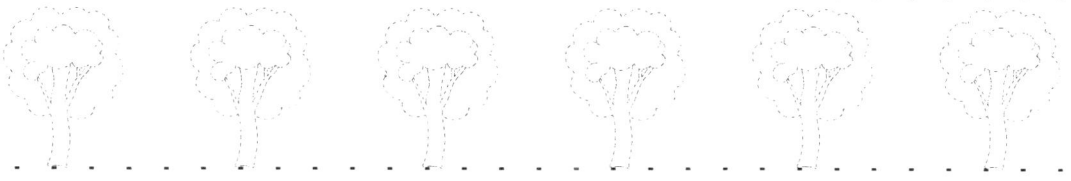

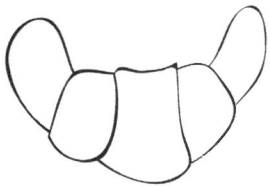

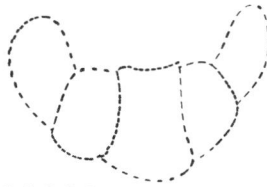

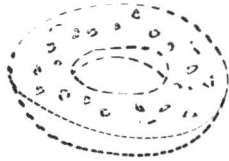

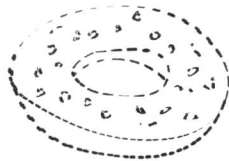

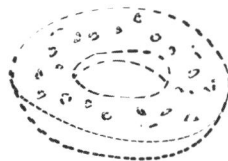

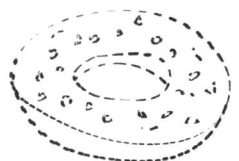

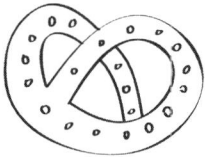

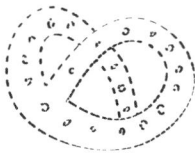

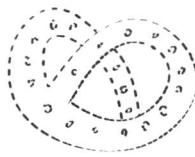

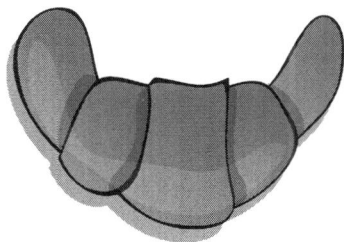

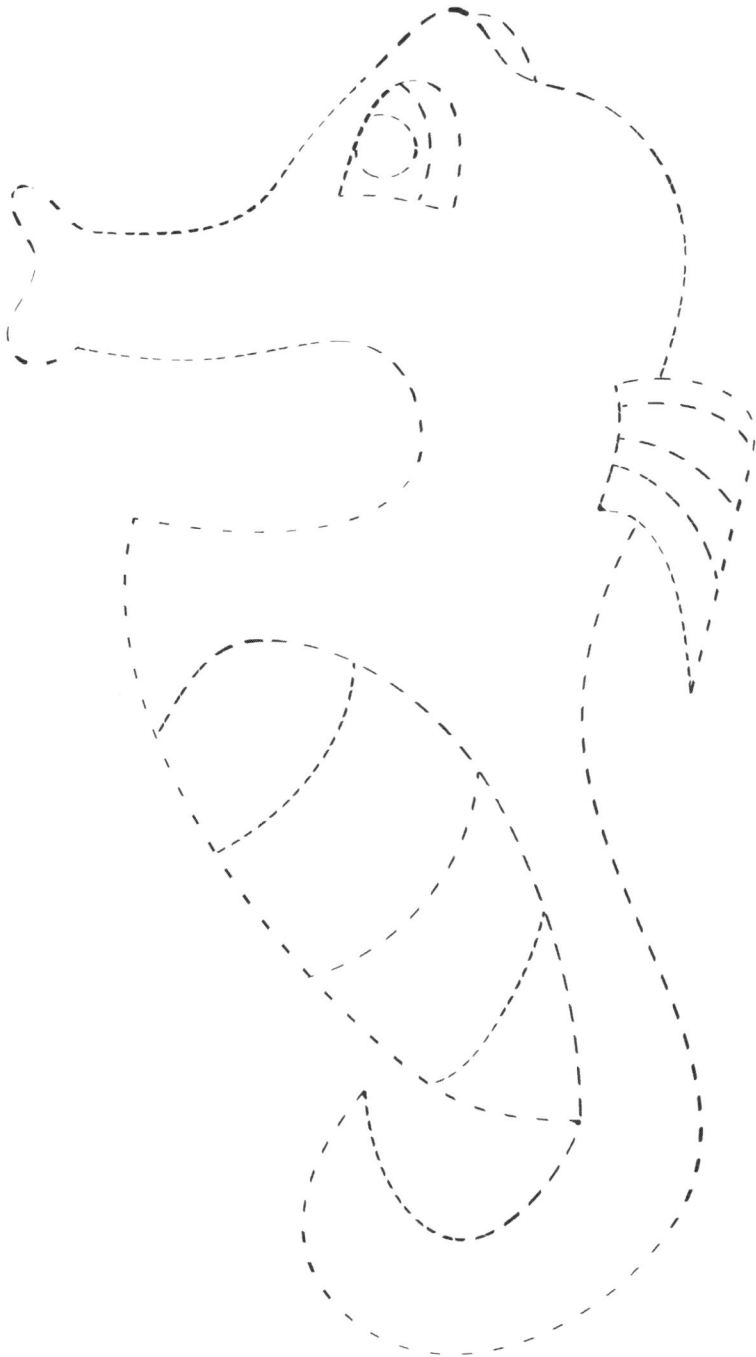

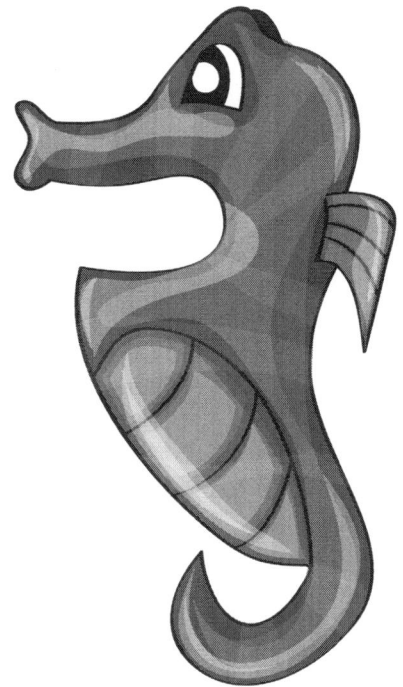

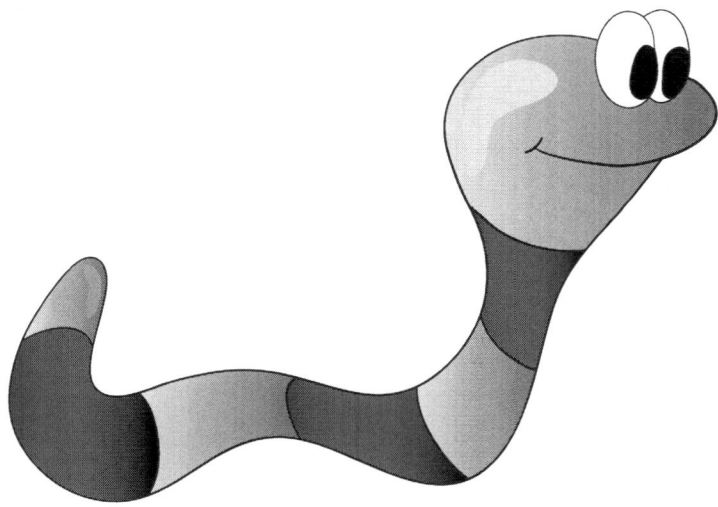

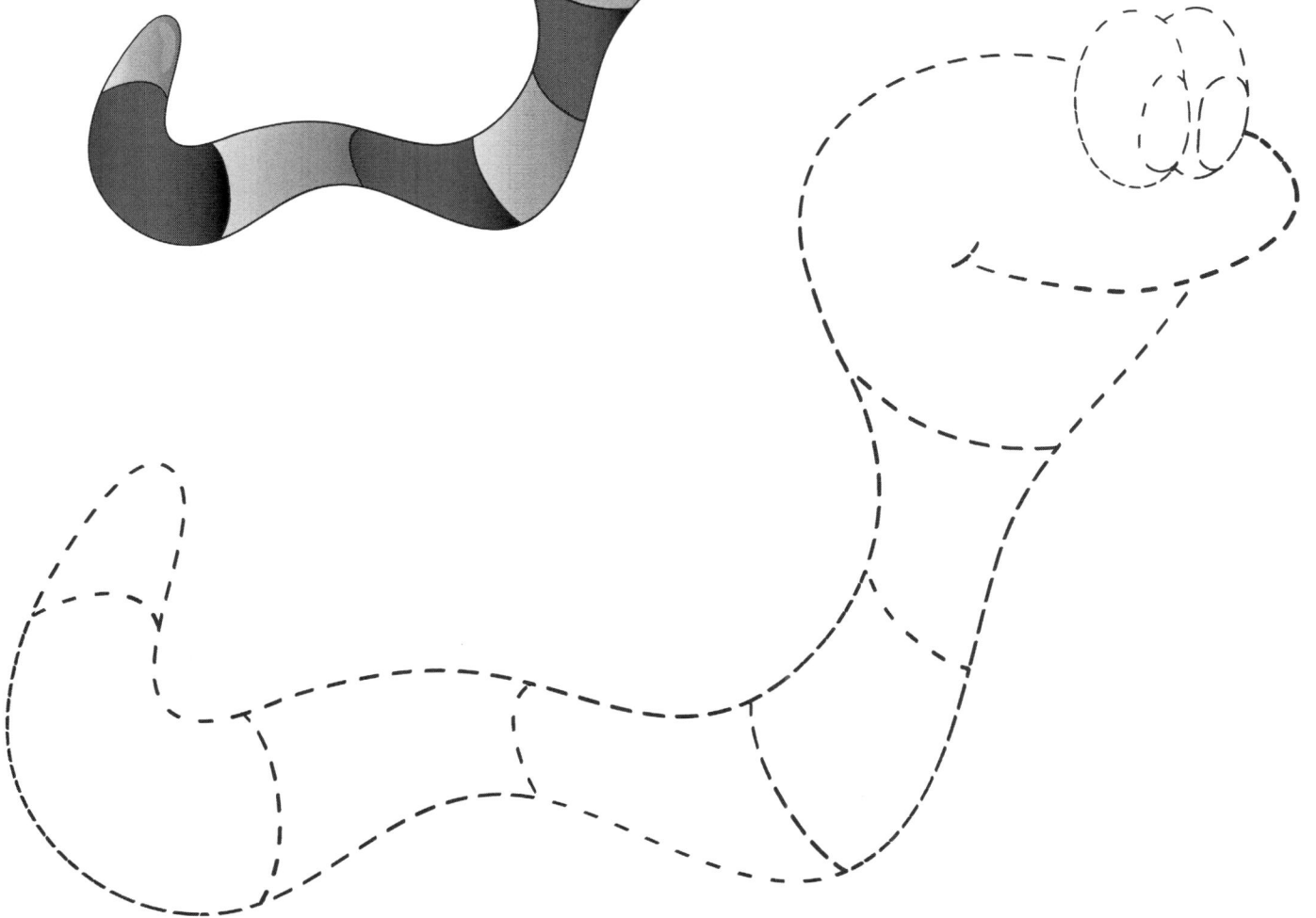

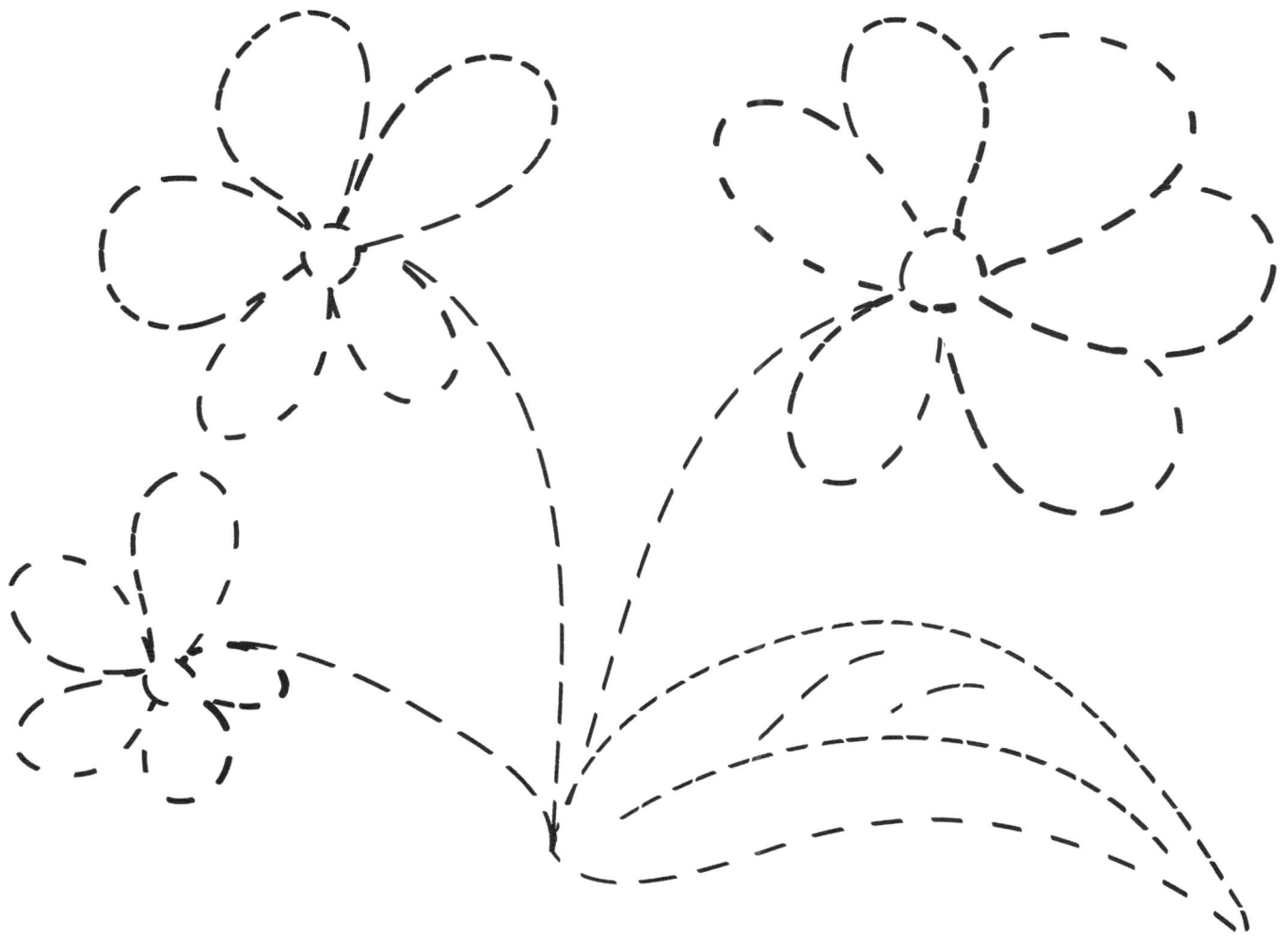

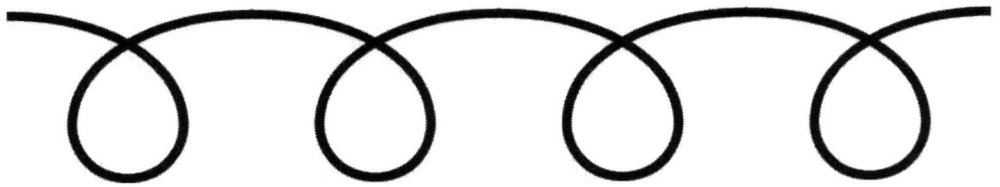

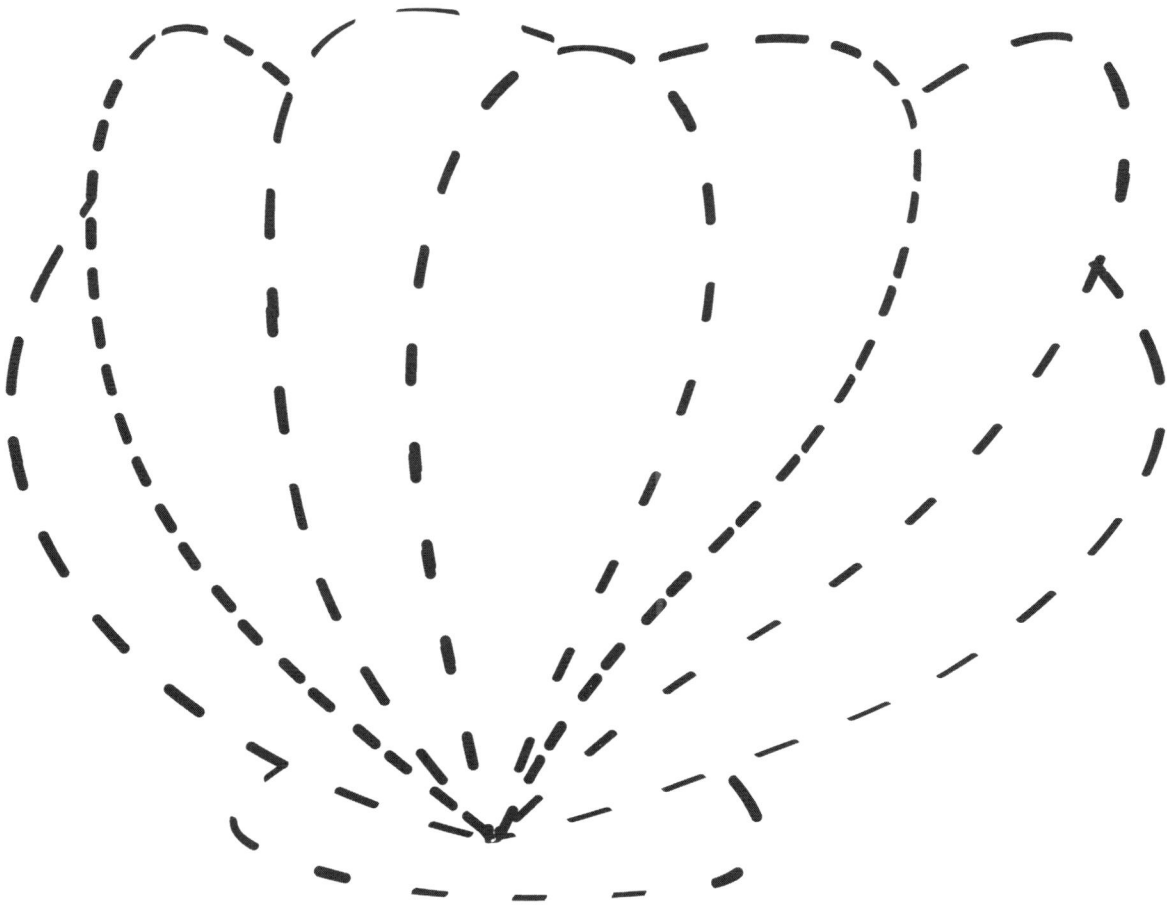

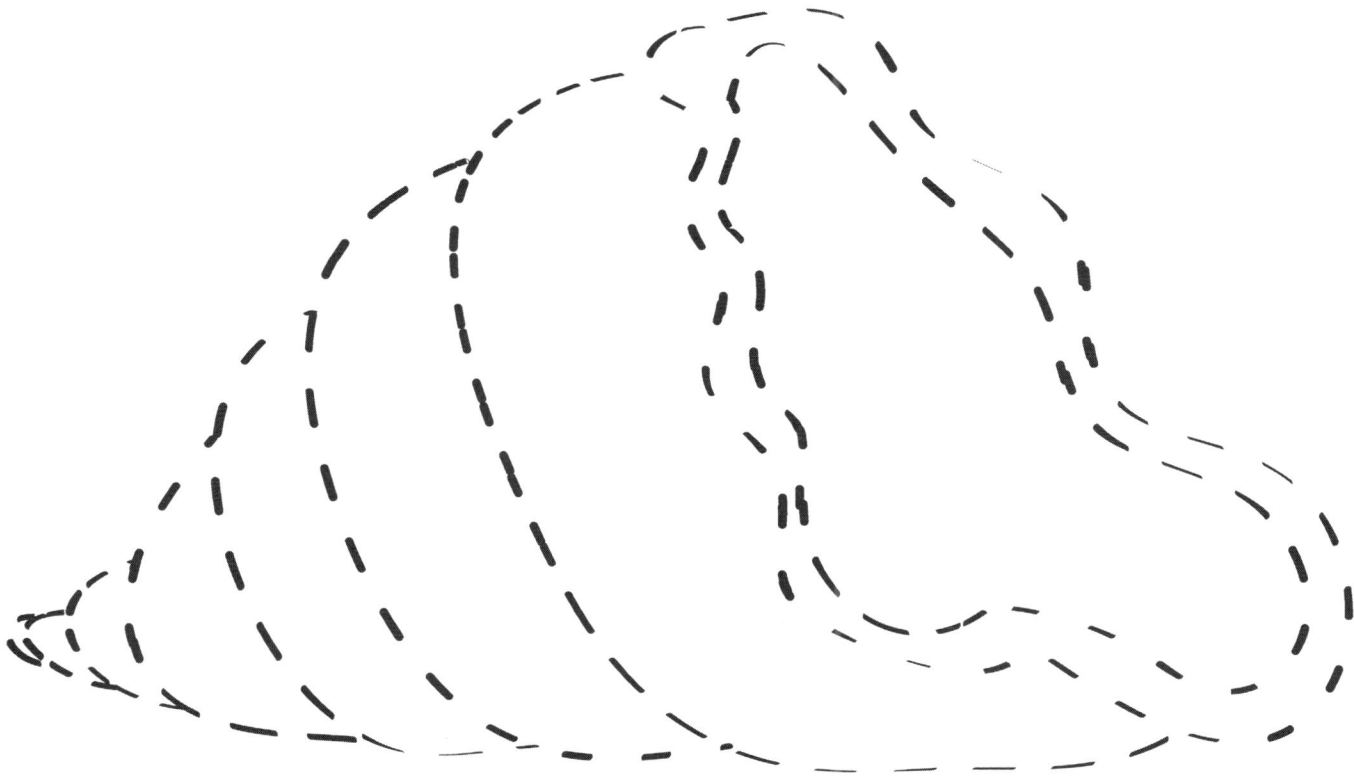

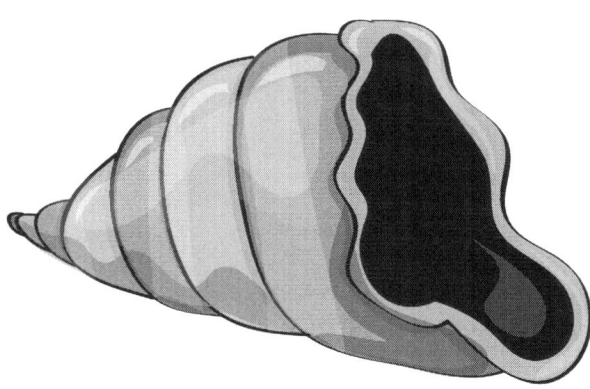

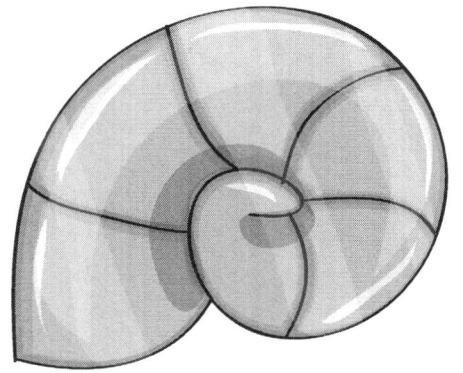

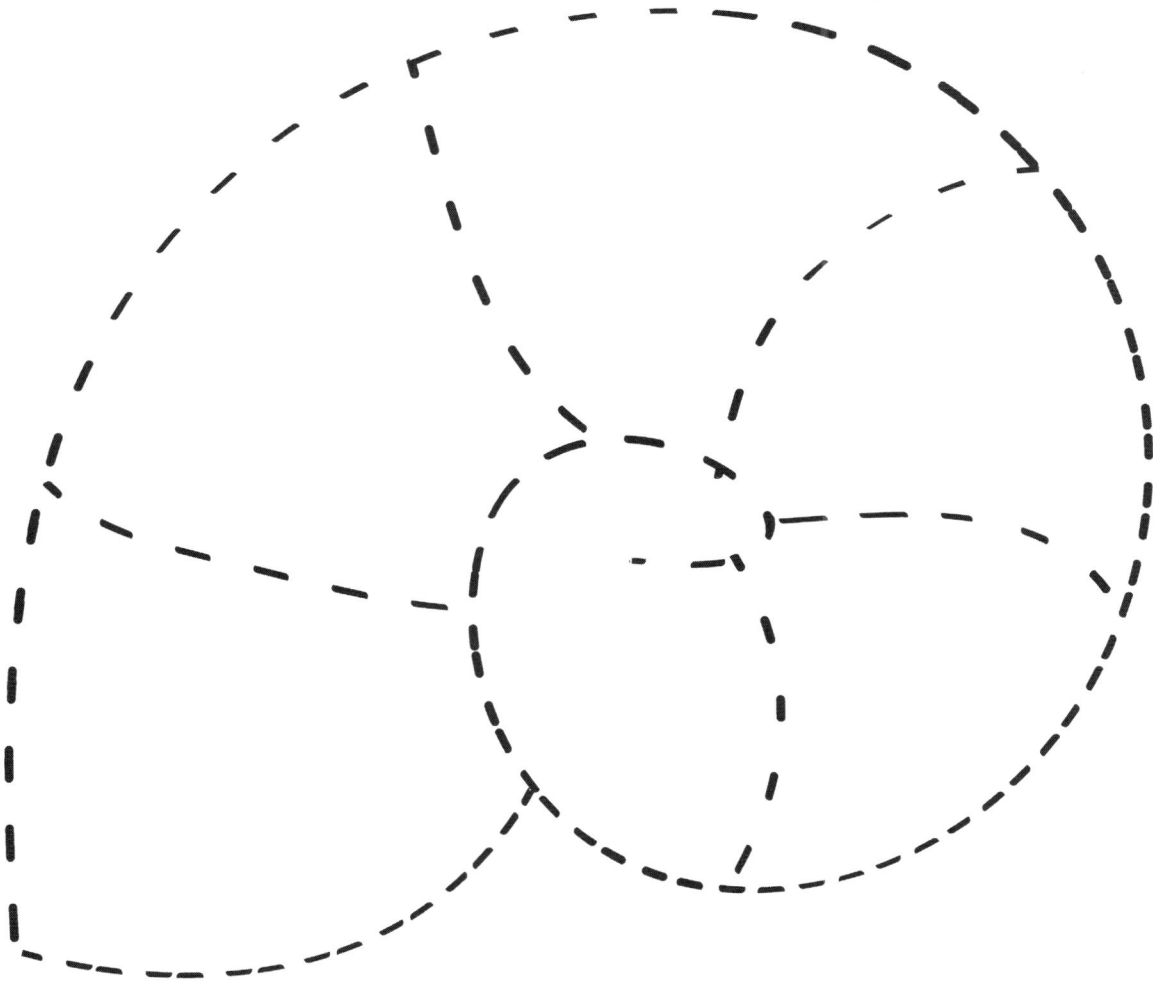

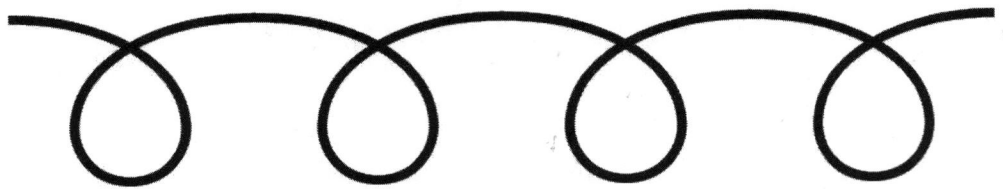

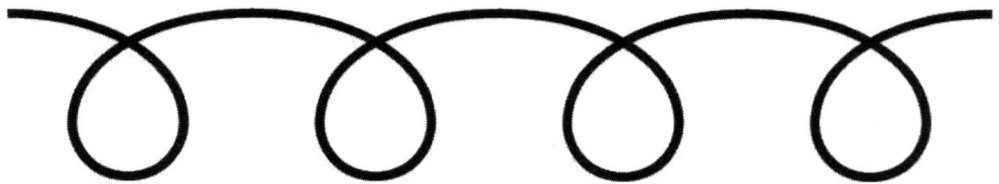

Printed in Great Britain
by Amazon.co.uk, Ltd.,
Marston Gate.